# LEARNING TO BE A WOMAN

Kenneth G. Smith
Floy M. Smith

Inter-Varsity Press
Downers Grove
Illinois 60515

*Tenth printing, February 1979*

© *1970 by Inter-Varsity Christian
Fellowship of the United States of
America. All rights reserved.
No part of this book may be
reproduced in any form without
written permission from
InterVarsity Press.*

*InterVarsity Press is the book-
publishing division of Inter-Varsity
Christian Fellowship, a student
movement active on campus
at hundreds of universities, colleges
and schools of nursing. For
information about local and regional
activities, write IVCF, 233 Langdon,
Madison, WI 53703.*

*Distributed in Canada through
InterVarsity Press, 1875 Leslie St.,
Unit 10, Don Mills, Ontario
M3B 2M5, Canada.*

*ISBN 0-87784-693-6
Library of Congress Catalog
Card Number: 78-120413*

*Printed in the United
States of America*

**table of contents**

*The book of Proverbs inquires, "Who can find a virtuous woman? for her price is far above rubies." It is still true. Such a woman is a rare gem.*

*Describe her any way you choose, a woman can only be called virtuous when she has come to understand . . . and enjoy . . . her role in life as God intended.*

*The design of this study, therefore, is to present an overview of woman as she is portrayed in the Scriptures. Woman as God designed her can only be understood and appreciated as she is viewed in terms of her position beside man. Here lies the secret to a woman's understanding of herself, not to mention her relating to others.*

*Yet today many women have lost this perspective. Commenting on one section of the parallel volume,* Learning to Be a Man, *Dr. Francis Schaeffer of L'Abri Fellowship in Switzerland observed, "It is curious how lost mankind so often moves to hurt itself. Surely this is the case in the States, where women's insistence on equal rights in a poor sense has brought them to the position of having fewer and fewer men who are men. And then the cycle continues and the women are hungry and hurt."*

*While a person could certainly make the study on her own, it has been in my mind that it would best be used in a group of half a dozen to a dozen women. Or, a small group of couples would also find it stimulating to share their studies section by section, the men following* Learning to Be a Man.

*If I were to recommend another volume to be used simultaneously with this study, it would be Shirley Rice's* The Christian Home: A Woman's View, *pub-*

*lished by the Tabernacle Church of Norfolk, 7120 Granby Street, Norfolk, Virginia 23505.*

*"A woman that feareth the Lord, she shall be praised," concludes God's Word. And this is the goal recommended for you who do this study.*

Kenneth G. Smith
Director, Board of Christian Education
Reformed Presbyterian Church of North America

## notes for the leader

Leading a Bible study can be an exciting experience! It's fascinating to watch God begin to reveal step by step what he wants to teach us. It's thrilling to see growth actually taking place. If a group of women enters into it with a readiness to learn and to obey what God makes known, this study will be no exception. And the results will be felt among those who count most—our families.

### the study itself

A clear understanding of the nature of the study will be of help. *Learning to Be a Woman* was designed to match the companion study, *Learning to Be a Man.* While a variety of studies for women is available, to a large extent they have been framed around the woman herself. This study on the other hand follows the example God set in the order of creation when he created woman from the first man. For that reason the entire study has been cast as it were in the framework of a man's point of view. After all, that's where woman lives her life. And that's where she finds her fulfillment. Many of the questions therefore deal with men. And so they must if a woman is to understand her role.

This is not essentially a "how to" book on Bible study, although the Scripture is the text and Bible study methods are employed. Nor is it intended to be a survey of Bible doctrine, although every unit deals with certain aspects of biblical truth. Finally the study does not attempt to present biblical psychology, although at times one will find related ideas coming up. *Learning to Be a Woman* seeks to give an integrated view of woman as the Bible describes her, so she can understand herself and function as a godly woman in her various relationships.

### how to use the study

First of all, don't be afraid of its length. And don't worry if it seems hard. As you'll find in the study, maturity requires responsibility and work. Growing Christians are not discouraged by something difficult. But they do lose interest in something too easy or canned. Women give themselves to decision-making and problem-solving every day. Don't turn them off by suggesting that following Christ is a perfunctory thing with no cost or challenge. Men who risk their lives for accomplishment are usually backed up by courageous wives encouraging them on. Enter the study therefore with abandon!

Next, recognize the value of personal investigation of the Scriptures, coupled with the benefits of talking over the answers. For best results, the study should be used with a group—in a church school class, a dorm study on campus, or a study for husbands and wives, the men using *Learning to Be a Man*.

This activity will be far from simply academic. Women must be stretched intellectually, but they also need to voice how they feel about things, honestly and openly. And they need to be confronted with their performance. Many questions, therefore, call for an opinion, and they will not always be easy to answer. They may be harder to share, particularly in a couples' study. A wise leader will at this point be discreet, but Christians, of all people, should be ready to assume responsibility for the opinions and life-style they embrace.

A number of different translations of the Scriptures were used in the preparation of the study, and you will find several called for at various points along the way. Broad translations or paraphrases will probably not be precise enough to pinpoint answers built upon particular words, but the standard and most common versions will be clear.

### some specific suggestions
Persons having led group studies will recognize the value of having an agreed-upon procedure for everyone in the group. Studies where only certain members actually work the assignment beforehand can have very poor results. The following suggestions have been used successfully with this study and are recommended:

**1.** Require that all assignments be completed in order to participate in discussion.
**2.** Give assignments in proportion to the time available for discussion. In most cases, a unit can be discussed in one hour, but even more time is desirable.
**3.** Do not go over each question and answer in the discussion. Select those you believe to be most significant for your group when making your preparation to lead.

**4.** Seek to establish the basic concept of each unit. In some cases this will be very explicit, in other cases implied.

**5.** Give opportunity to share the opinion questions which deal with life performance. Where questions are particularly personal, consider dividing into groups of two and let the women talk face to face. Encourage them to pray for each other and to respect confidences.

**6.** Do not teach. Let people share their ideas and findings, taking opportunity to summarize at the end of the discussion. Even this can be delegated, for example, "Nancy, how would you summarize our discussion?"

**about unit 19**
The point of this concluding unit focuses on a woman's making use of the Scripture in her daily life . . . and learning how. It is suggested that the leader give a topical assignment for the women to work out and share: for example, faith. Then, try one of the character studies in the same manner. This could very well lead to a continuation of the group for an unlimited time around direct Bible study. Generally speaking, it takes a bit of time to learn how to work out the kind of personal application called for in these studies. But the fellowship becomes most valuable when this kind of application tops off a discussion of the objective truths of God's Word.

unit

# 1 A LOOK AT A HAPPY WOMAN

hap•pi•ness   'hap-i-nəs   *n.* 1 *obs*: good fortune: PROSPERITY 2a: a state of well-being and contentment: JOY b: a pleasurable satisfaction 3: APTNESS, FELICITY                    *(Webster's Seventh New Collegiate Dictionary)*

It is the intent of this book to help you as a *woman* realize in your life the fulfillment of God's purpose for you, and therefore his blessing. Logically, then, we turn to the center of his Word to Psalm 1 which begins with the word *blessed* or, in our language, *happy*.

How to achieve *fulfillment* and *enjoy* life confronts every woman every day of her existence. Some women have found true happiness, which among other things proves that such a condition is possible. But the question is "How?"

"Happiness," as the above definition shows, means "well-being"—knowing and feeling it. Many women, however, find their lives "haphazard," that is, "marked by lack of plan, order, or direction: aimless." They neither believe they are in a state of well-being nor enjoy the contentment which comes with accomplishment. They are in fact haphazard.

There is a real connection between happiness and accomplishment. According to the Bible, you have been created by God for a purpose, and your happiness depends upon your fitting into that plan. But you must fit in as a *woman*.

Now read slowly Psalm 1.

This introduction to the book of Psalms puts all persons into one of two groups. How would you describe these groups?

Group 1 _____

Group 2 _____

How are these two groups described in the New Testament? (See John 3:36.)

Group 1 _____

Group 2 _____

The person *not* in harmony with God is described as being very easily swayed and unstable. What expression in Psalm 1:4 suggests this?

_____

As you think back over your own life, what are some of the desires and frustrations which have tended to "blow you around"?

_____

_____

_____

_____

Now read again verses 1-3. Here is a description of the person, or for our purposes the woman, who is in a relationship with God. No longer uncommitted or wishy-washy, she has a mind-set which determines her life. She is described first of all as *blessed* or *in a state of well-being*.

With the power of negative thinking in her life, how would such a woman be described according to verse 1?

_____

_____

_____

(Optional: for a brief comparison, note *sit* in Ephesians 2:6, *walk* in Ephesians 2:10, and *stand* in Ephesians 6:13.)

A balanced woman, according to Scripture, has both negative and positive emphases in her life. In verse 2 what is the positive emphasis?

_____

_____

_____

Look up the word *delight* in a dictionary and write down the definition.

_____

_____

According to Joshua 1:8, what is the real purpose or objective in *meditating* on God's Word?

_____

_____

_____

God spoke these things to a person with responsibility. Why do you suppose God would tell Joshua the key to success was his meditation on and obedience to what God told him?

_____

_____

_____

To establish more definitely that God's Word must have top priority in a *blessed* person's life, check on the following people. Both men and women are included since the principle is universal. Write down the expression which shows their regard for God's Word.

Jeremiah (a prophet) in Jeremiah 15:16 _____

_____

Lydia (a business woman) in Acts 16:14 _____

_____

Job (a businessman) in Job 23:12 _____

_____

Mary (an engaged girl) in Luke 1:38 _____

_____

Mary (a friend of Jesus) in Luke 10:38-42 _____

_____

Many persons call themselves Christians and easily suggest they live by the Sermon on the Mount. In contrast to this, what requirement does Jesus lay down regarding his Word in the final paragraph of that sermon? You will find it in Matthew 7:24-27.

_____

_____

Now go back and meditate on Psalm 1:3. To show the well-being of the blessed man, the Scripture uses the figure of a *tree*. What do these illustrations suggest to you about a blessed woman?

*planted by the rivers of water* _____

_____

*brings forth his fruit in his season* _____

_____

*his leaf shall not wither* _____

_____

The final expression in verse 3 is a comprehensive description. Compare it with Joshua 1:8. What difference do you see between the prosperity described here and the success for which most people work?

_____

_____

**an honest look at myself**
Check as many as you feel are true about yourself:
**1.** I would presently describe my *delight* in the Scriptures to be
_____very low _____ moderate _____ good _____ very high
**2.** This condition resulted because
_____ I had much help in learning how to read and study God's Word.
_____ I have never had much help in learning how to take in God's Word.
_____ I seem to have trouble understanding much of the Bible.
_____ From early childhood I have really enjoyed the Scriptures.
_____ Frankly, I don't *like* to read the Bible!
_____ Since my conversion, God has given me a hunger for the Scriptures.
_____ Somehow I am not sure about whether I'm a real Christian or not.
_____ Other: _____

**3.** In order to get a greater *knowledge* of God's Word each week, I am using the following means:
_____ worship service(s)
_____ church school class
_____ daily Bible reading
_____ regular Bible study (personal or group)
_____ daily family worship
_____ plan of Scripture memory
_____ other: _____

**4.** At present which of the above do you consider to be most productive in affecting your life?

_____

**5.** To be able to appropriate God's Word for herself, a woman must have some "know-how." Check, in the spaces below, the statements which you feel describe your own needs.

_____ I need to learn the whole thing from scratch.

_____ I think I know what to do, but have trouble organizing my time to get it in.

_____ I need some personal help in

_____ my reading of Scripture

_____ my Bible study

_____ memorizing Scripture

_____ My know-how in applying Scripture is weak.

_____ I think I'm generally okay on know-how, but I need time to share with other persons how I'm doing.

_____ Other: _____

**6.** Perhaps the greatest evidence to a woman that she is a Christian—or in a state of well-being—can be seen in how God is changing her *character*. As you reflect on your life, name two areas which have been undergoing change by the Holy Spirit.

a. _____

b. _____

**7.** Publishing women's magazines is big business today. Look through one of your favorites and select (cut it out) a picture of a woman who according to the magazine "has everything." What features do you see? What appeal has been used? How do you feel about this kind of woman?

_____

_____

_____

In the next chapters, we will look into God's Word to see what he says about *being a woman*. But basic to consulting him on this or any subject is an attitude of prompt response to whatever he may say. To learn from God involves a mind-set of readiness to obey.

unit
## AS HIS CREATURE

"What a beautiful baby! She looks just like her mother, doesn't she?"

And so with simple and pleasurable insight, people identify a new baby with its parents. Having known the father and mother, they can immediately recognize the same light or dark complexion, the same shape of the nose, or similarities in the smile of the child. In other words, the parents' characteristics help us identify their children.

It's not strange then to find that a hard look at what the Scripture says about God explains much of what we know about his "offspring." The Bible simply says that life itself came from God and that he created man. To understand what it means to "be a woman" requires a review of man's origin and purpose. To do this, we must go back to the beginning . . . and God.

Some people, when they pick up a book, turn to the last chapter to see how it ends. But no writer expects the reader to grasp the conclusion until he understands the beginning. The Bible also has a beginning, and without an understanding of the first three chapters of Genesis, a person can only gain a sketchy idea of the rest of God's Word.

Before trying to answer the following questions, read over the first three chapters of Genesis.
_____ Check here when you have finished.

**man's origin***
Where did the whole idea of "man" come from? (Genesis 1:26) (Compare this with Job 38:3, 4; Job 40:7, 8; Ephesians 1:11b.)

_____

How does Scripture explain the sexes? (Genesis 1:27)

_____

What are some of the things this implies about a woman's attitude toward sex?

_____

_____

**man's purpose**
In Genesis 1:28 the Scripture states that the first thing God did for his human creatures was to "bless" them. What do you think this means in light of our study in Psalm 1?

_____

_____

In general, the responsibilities listed in Genesis 1:28 are grouped into two categories. Do you agree with this? If so, name these two duties. If not, list them as you see them.

_____

_____

Converting these overall purposes into specifics, what did they mean to Adam?

In Genesis 2:5 _____

*The term _man_ is frequently used generically, and not necessarily just in terms of the masculine.

In Genesis 2:15 _____

In Genesis 2:20 _____

Note in 2:18 why God made "woman." In the light of man's purpose, what does this say about his responsibility toward his wife?

_____

What does this say about her responsibility to her husband?

_____

The relationship between man's basic "make-up" and his purpose is graphically shown in Genesis 2:19. Read this over again.

What work was Adam doing?_____

_____

What did he have to do to carry it out?_____

_____

Who "thought up" the names? _____

How does this relate to God's "thinking up" creating man? (Cf. 1:26)

_____

Can you see a similarity between man and God in being "creative"? Explain what you think it is.

_____

_____

(Actually man and woman are more imitative than creative, but they function like God or in this sense "after his image.")

Suppose a woman refuses or neglects her responsibility. What does this say about her concept of herself?

_____

_____

What does it do to her as an individual?   _____

_____

### man's problem
Being God's creatures, man and woman were in a relationship with God. How was that relationship described in Genesis 2:16, 17?

_____

What specific purpose did God have in creating woman? (Genesis 2:18)

_____

Instead of this what did she do? (Genesis 3:6)

_____

Facing the test of their loyalty to God, Adam and Eve exercised their wills. But when confronted with the responsibility of their choice, how did they act? (Genesis 3:12, 13; check also I Timothy 2:13, 14 before you answer.)

_____

_____

The effects of irresponsibility immediately confronted mankind. Read Genesis 3:14-24.

How was man affected?   _____

_____

How was woman affected? _____

_____

In summarizing this section, read Psalm 8.
_____ Check here when finished.

Man by virtue of creation by God possesses a "make-up" in many ways similar to God's. Not the least of these is his position as "ruler" over the created world. But because of sin, man finds it hard (actually impossible) to be what God intended. He must have help, and that help must meet his need to be restored to his original position, where once again he can experience God's blessing on his life and work.

**what this means to me**
Using the scale 1 as good, 2 as average, and 3 as needing attention, how would you rate your present functioning as a woman?
_____ I respond to responsibility.
_____ I like work that stretches me beyond my experience.
_____ I like my husband's taking the leadership in my family.
_____ I have a clear understanding of my position in terms of God's call on my life.
_____ I assume the blame for my own mistakes.
_____ I work at this thing of being a woman.
_____ I am confident of God's blessing on my life and work.

Look back on your childhood and recall what "chores" you had as your regular responsibility. (Indicate if you had pets or animals to care for.)

_____

_____

_____

_____

_____

Think through your present responsibilities. Of all that you have to do, what gives you the most satisfaction? Indicate why you think this is true.

_____

_____

_____

_____

unit

AS HIS CHILD

To know . . . and feel . . . that one has been carefully planned and created by God as a unique creature designed for an important work has much to do with a woman's sense of well-being. It is basic to being a woman.

However, since woman chose to exercise her will out of harmony with God and his purpose for her, woman has brought upon herself all the effects of her "rebellion." You can read for yourself what happens to people when they refuse to treat God as God. It is plainly shown in Romans 1. But as you ponder this portion of Scripture, note the expressions showing how *God gave them up*, or simply left them to their own imaginations.

Read slowly Romans 1:18-32.
_____ Check here when finished.

To recognize the relevance of this description of mankind, take today's newspaper and analyze just the front page. How many of the articles deal with problems specifically mentioned in Romans 1?_____

In passing, observe in Romans 1:26, 27 that one of the effects of this rebellion can be homosexuality, that is, men and women no longer acting and feeling normal. In the light of growing numbers of practicing homosexuals, it is important to understand that the root of this perversion in a woman lies in her failure to be the person God created her to be. And of course one of the by-products is the frustration of *knowing* she is not what she should be.

However, what does the Scripture say about a person *in Christ*? (II Corinthians 5:17)

_____

Now read verse 15 and explain the answer you just wrote down.

_____

_____

**man as a "son"**
Every person is a created being. Nothing can alter that. However, when a person becomes a *new creation* in Christ, the Bible describes the new relationship to God in terms of "sonship." The following study is designed to help you grasp what that relationship means and how it affects being a woman.

Jesus told a story to illustrate God's love for people. It has become popularly known as the parable of "The Prodigal Son." If you cannot define "prodigal," look it up in a dictionary.

Read this parable in Luke 15:11-32.
_____ Check here when finished.

What is the attitude of the younger son at the beginning of the story?

_____

In verses 17-19, how has his attitude changed?

_____

In spite of this different attitude toward himself, how does his father treat him?
_____ as a servant _____ as a son
Give supporting reasons for your choice.

_____

_____

Why do you suppose the older brother is angry?

_____

_____

What "image" does he have of his relationship with his father (see also 15:2)?
_____ a son serving in love
_____ a servant feeling only drudgery

Why should this cause him to reject his brother?

_____

_____

As you read this story, how do you find yourself feeling about the father?

_____

_____

The father/son relationship pictured in this parable describes the actual relation-ship which exists between a person and God when the person becomes a *new creature* in Christ. It has a great bearing on one's confidence and enjoyment. As a "restored" creature, a "son" or "daughter" possesses in Christ the ability and the desire to fulfill God's original purpose for him or her. As one thinks of God and thinks of himself, he thinks of "sonship."

In Galatians 4:4-7:
What term is used to describe Jesus Christ? _____

What was his purpose in dying on the cross? _____

_____

What evidence does the Christian have of his own sonship? _____

_____

What else accompanies that sonship? _____

_____

In Romans 8:14-17, what else characterizes this child/father relationship?

_____

_____

In Jude 20, 21 there is a direct instruction to *keep yourselves in the love of God.*
What three other instructions relate to this?

1. _____

2. _____

3. _____

To summarize, the relationship of God to man and woman as described in
Scripture begins with creation. Man and woman, by virtue of their creation by
God and by virtue of God's own appointment, have status over all other things.

But as sinners, they must now be restored by the death and resurrection of
Christ. All who are so restored are now called *children of God*, and they experience a relationship far beyond that of "servants." The child/father relationship
means many things; but essential to it is the integration of acceptance and
responsibility. In Christ, a woman can once again think, feel, and act like a
woman—in ready fellowship with her Father in heaven, and with satisfaction in
her work.

### thinking it over
The Bible describes the "family" idea as an illustration of the relationship an
individual enjoys with God. See Ephesians 3:15. Write a paragraph about your
childhood. What relationship did you have with your parents? your brothers?
your sisters?

_____

_____

_____

_____

Try to recall your father's life and background. Go as far back in his childhood as you can, and be specific about persons, places, and things. What could you tell your children about him?

If you were to describe your relationship with God at the present time in the light of the Prodigal Son story, where would you put yourself?

_____ The younger son wanting to leave home

_____ The younger son alone and wanting to go home

_____ The younger son enjoying the blessings of real sonship

_____ The older brother faithfully doing his work

_____ The older brother resentful he had not had a party

_____ The older brother refusing his brother's fellowship

_____ Other: _____

Jude 20, 21 gives specific instructions or means for keeping ourselves in the love of God. As you consider your relationship to your heavenly Father, which of these is most needed in your life right now? (Put it in your own words.)

_____

_____

What can/will you do about it?

_____

_____

While a woman may recognize the fact of her being a child of God, she may not feel that kinship. In order to cultivate that feeling, she must *act* like a daughter.

What are you doing now to cultivate this family relationship with God? What ought you to begin doing?

_____

_____

_____

_____

unit

WHAT I "LOOK" LIKE

Enjoying life as a woman certainly requires an understanding of what a woman is: a created being who in Christ becomes a daughter of her heavenly Father. So John writes, "Behold what manner of love the Father hath bestowed on us, that we should be called the children of God. . . ."

God's Word clearly states a woman has a relationship to herself, as well as to God.

Read what Jesus said in Matthew 22:35-40. In verse 39, what two words reveal that a person does have a relationship to himself?

_____

What word in that verse describes what a woman's attitude toward herself should be? _____

In this passage (including verse 37) there are three objects of a person's love. Put them in their logical sequence.

First _____

Second _____

Third _____

A woman's relationship to herself, if it is biblical, builds upon a true and unvarnished understanding of *who* she is, not just *what* she is. How did the following women reply when they identified themselves?

Rebekah—Genesis 24:23, 24 _____

_____

Ruth—Ruth 3:8, 9 _____

_____

Mary—Luke 1:38_____

_____

How do you reply when you are asked, "Who are you?" _____

_____

While on the surface a woman is identified by her name and address, she comes to the position of "loving" herself only when she really knows and accepts herself as she is. So she must *look* at herself.

**what I "look" like**
When the psalmist thought of himself, in Psalm 139:14-16, how did he respond?

_____

_____

Do you think this is being realistic? Explain.

_____

_____

It's an interesting and significant factor that Scripture so often describes persons in physical terms. Notice the following and indicate the physical quality(ies) portrayed.

Ehud—Judges 3:15_____

Moses—Deuteronomy 34:7 _____

Job's daughters—Job 42:15 _____

Eli—I Samuel 4:18 _____

David—I Samuel 16:12 _____

Sarah—Genesis 12:11 _____

Abigail—I Samuel 25:3 _____

Elisha—II Kings 2:23, 24 _____

Absalom—II Samuel 14:25, 26 _____

Mephibosheth—II Samuel 9:13 _____

Zaccheus—Luke 19:3 _____

Jesus (then)—Isaiah 53:2 _____

Jesus (now)—Revelation 1:12-16 _____

Why do you suppose God included these physical descriptions in the Scripture?

_____

_____

While the apostle Paul wrestled with a doctrinal question in this passage, what root principle may be found for our purposes in Romans 9:20, 21?

_____

_____

In Paul's own case it is likely he had some physical problem. In II Corinthians 12:7-10 what attitude does he take toward this problem?

_____

_____

Learning to accept and capitalize on what I look like poses one side. I Corinthians 6:19, 20 brings out the other. What is it?

_____

_____

How should this principle affect a woman's concern for her appearance?

_____

**a second look**
In general how do you feel about your appearance? Does it bother you?

_____

_____

Some things we can change. What for example is your plan of physical fitness?

_____

When was the last time you had a physical examination? _____

Do you have regular check-ups? _____

Name one thing you could do to improve your physical condition and appearance. Is there any reason you can't start doing it now?

_____

Being womanly does not mean being physically beautiful. Rather it means being aware of the person God made me to be, accepting who I am and exercising myself to be as physically pleasing to God, myself and others as I can.

unit

WHAT I "THINK"

When the Scripture says, "of the abundance of the heart his mouth speaketh" (Luke 6:45), it becomes apparent that at the root of a person's being is conviction. What a woman thinks determines what she is and does.

Therefore it's not surprising to find Jesus stating in the "greatest commandment" the germ of this truth. How does he say it in Matthew 22:37?

---

**what I "think"**
The fact is that most women do have opinions about all kinds of things. But opinions may be wrong. They must be built on the facts. How do the following passages bring out a person's responsibility to get the facts?

Romans 12:2 _____

Ephesians 4:14, 15 _____

II Peter 3:18 _____

Proverbs 4:7, 13 _____

All knowledge of course is not contained in the Scriptures. What influence do the Scriptures have on a person's thinking? (II Timothy 3:15-17)

---

What effect might God's Word have on a woman in terms of her thinking about her daily work?

_____

_____

_____

People who can make good decisions are hard to come by. What advantage did David as a king have with the men of Issachar on his staff? (I Chronicles 12:32)

_____

The book of Proverbs contains much about "thinking." In Proverbs 17:27, 28 what are some of the marks of wisdom?

_____

_____

What are some other marks in James 3:17?    _____

_____

This idea of right thinking in the Word of God always relates knowledge to its application in the life of a woman, not just in her mind. How is this seen in Psalm 111:10?

_____

_____

How a woman *really* thinks therefore may not show up in the amount of education she has, but rather in how she applies herself to what she knows ... and is learning. This can be seen clearly in Paul's analysis in I Corinthians 13:11, the "love" chapter. What happened when Paul became a man?

_____

What would you say about a woman who had a great amount of knowledge but demonstrated very little personal discipline?

_____

_____

Look then at how Jesus approached the matter of learning. In the following passages what requirement is necessary in order to "know"?

John 7:17 _____

John 8:31, 32 _____

John 3:20, 21 _____

How is this same principle seen in Matthew 4:19?

_____

_____

As a result of their experience with Jesus and filling by the Holy Spirit, the apostles demonstrated no fear about being misunderstood or opposed. But what surprised their critics in Acts 4:13?

_____

In summary, God expects a woman to love him by using her mental capacities. But according to Scripture, being intellectually sharp is not in itself a virtue. Every woman must apply truth to her life. Then her life will begin to show the qualities of true wisdom and maturity.

**"thinking" about it**
Why do some women fear giving their opinions in a group?

_____

_____

Not everyone has the same mental abilities. How do you think a woman should determine her own? (Do you think she should?)

_____

_____

List below five books outside of the Bible that have influenced your life. Explain how.

1. _____

_____

2. _____

_____

3. _____

_____

4. _____

_____

5. _____

_____

What three factors would you list as the most influential in contributing to mental laziness?

_____

_____

_____

How familiar are you with the constitution–the thinking–of your church?

_____ I don't know what it is.

_____ I know what it is but I haven't read it.

_____ I've read it but I haven't studied it.

_____ I've studied it to a considerable degree.

unit

HOW I "FEEL"

"Hey, Sue, did you see Jill this morning?"

"Yeah. Wonder what's buggin' her?"

"I dunno, but one look at her is enough."

"She'd better talk to somebody. This business of just clamming up doesn't solve anything."

"Well, she's obviously unhappy. It shows in her face."

A basically happy woman has a good relationship with herself. Remember Psalm 1? The description of the person there portrayed is "blessed," or "happy." And while this basically is a state of well-being, it also involves "feeling" that condition. One of the by-products of a true relationship with Christ comes in the area of "feelings" or emotions. Look at this in Scripture.

**how I "feel"**
To begin with, the Christian woman can be sure of certain things about the area of her emotions. Read II Timothy 1:6, 7.

What has the Christian received? _____

_____

What feeling described here is *not* of God? _____

The King James Version uses the term "sound mind" in verse 7. Check another translation and record what you find.

_____

Paul reminds Timothy that as a Christian he has not received the "spirit" of fear. Instead a Christian receives the Holy Spirit (Romans 8:9b). Read now Galatians 5:22, 23 and then list below what the Holy Spirit brings with him when he enters a woman.

_____    _____    _____

_____    _____    _____

_____    _____    _____

Go back and circle the ones you believe affect how a Christian woman "feels."

The last item mentioned in the King James Version is "temperance." Look this up in another translation and compare it with "sound mind" in II Timothy 1:7. What do you find?

_____

_____

There is an important principle taught here in this matter of self-control. It is a common idea that a woman is not responsible for how she feels, and that feelings control her. However, in I Corinthians 14:32 the apostle Paul—in dealing with a particular problem in the church—unequivocally states a different principle. What is it?

_____

The same principle shows itself in Psalm 43. As Dr. D. Martyn Lloyd-Jones suggests, does the psalmist in his depression "listen to himself" or does he "talk to himself"? (See verse 5.)

_____

We conclude therefore that part of this matter of being a woman pertains to her feelings, and that maturity includes self-control or mastering our feelings, rather than being mastered by them.

It is not therefore immature to have feelings. This is a good thing since God has made us as emotional beings. Nor is it wrong to express feelings. This can be shown by the countless examples of emotion in the Bible. Some references are listed below. Look them up, record *who* was involved, *what* emotion was expressed, and *how* it showed.

Luke 10:33, 34 _____

Matthew 27:18 _____

Mark 14:72 _____

Genesis 3:7-10 _____

Luke 7:37, 38 _____

_____

I Chronicles 15:27-29 (cf. II Samuel 6:20-23) _____

_____

Acts 5:41, 42 _____

These are just a few instances, but you will notice them all through Scripture. True to life, the Bible shows people as having emotions. And they are expressed.

Which of the following statements do you think is most nearly correct? Support your choice with reasons.

_____ Emotions are good and by all means should be expressed.

_____ Emotions are good, but it is not necessary to express them.

_____ Emotions, while created by God, have been affected by sin and therefore must be controlled, sometimes by expression, sometimes by suppression.

_____ Some emotions are good and some are not. One should express the good and suppress the bad.

Reasons: _____

_____

Some of Satan's most vicious attacks on the Christian come in this sphere. What name is Satan given in Revelation 12:10? _____

Now in the light of this aspect of Satan's activity, read again Matthew 22:39. What is the standard by which you are to *love your neighbor*? _____

Suppose under Satan's attacks you develop an attitude of always "accusing" or condemning yourself. How will this inevitably show in your relations to others?

_____

According to Romans 8:31-34, is a self-condemning attitude a sign of Christian virtue? _____

What then should we *do* according to Hebrews 4:14-16? _____

_____

When Jesus had finished washing his disciples' feet, he taught them a lesson. On what principle did the emotional feeling involved depend? (John 13:17)

_____

In summary, a woman becomes a woman as she learns about her feelings and how to express and control them. In Christ she is given the Holy Spirit who in turn gives a proper sense of well-being characterized by holiness. The expression of emotion depends, therefore, on whether the Holy Spirit has given it or whether Satan has provoked it. The Christian woman thus seeks to discipline herself under the Holy Spirit's control and to resist Satan with his self-critical attacks. The Christian woman *acts* on what God says, whether she *feels* like it or not. Obedience leads to happiness.

*Special note:* The Bible notes that sometimes the Christian experiences feelings of dismay and grief because of his identity with Jesus Christ in a sinful world and not as a direct result of his own disobedience. One of the most significant illustrations of this can be felt in Psalm 44. Read the entire psalm, and then note verse 22—the reason for the psalmist's plight.

Now compare this with Romans 8. After dealing with the crossfire a Christian encounters, Paul the apostle quotes from Psalm 44. See verse 36. The feelings accompanying suffering for Christ are real! But even here the apostle demonstrates a self-control (or a Spirit-control) built upon a persuasion about God's truth. Hence, the victory of verses 37-39!

**getting the "feel" of it**
Why do people, particularly in Western culture, cover up their feelings of sorrow and think it a sign of weakness to cry?

_____

_____

_____

What relationship exists between a church that expresses its feelings and a church that's growing?

_____

_____

How would you assess your church in this regard?

_____

_____

Describe the feelings you have toward yourself that tend to "get you down."

_____

_____

_____

Have you searched out what Scripture has to say about these feelings and how to overcome them? Do you know how to make such a study?

_____

Which of the questions in this section **how I "feel"** was most significant you you? Why?

_____

_____

_____

unit

# WHAT I CAN "DO"

Early in this study it was pointed out that there is a direct connection between happiness (or the state of well-being) and accomplishment. The completion or fulfillment of an assignment brings with it a sense of satisfaction, and generally there follows a desire to move ahead into the next venture.

**what can I do?**
This built-in drive has its origin in the nature of man and woman. How is this seen in Genesis 1:26-28?

_____

Although both sexes share in this pursuit, what is woman's unique role according to Genesis 2:18?

_____

The Scripture also has much to say about persons who do *not* exercise themselves in this responsibility. What principles do you see in these passages?

Proverbs 24:30-34 _____

_____

Proverbs 10:4, 5 _____

_____

II Thessalonians 3:10-12 _____

_____

In the light of this God-given purpose, a woman then considers what she *can* do. Below are listed some people included in Scripture. See if you can remember what the Bible says about their abilities. Look them up if you need to.

Bezaleel (Exodus 31:1-5)_____

_____

Daniel (Daniel 1:3-6)_____

_____

Chenaniah (I Chronicles 15:22) _____

David (I Samuel 16:17, 18) _____

_____

Joseph (Genesis 39:3, 4; 39:21, 22; 41:38-40) _____

_____

Aholiab (Exodus 38:23) _____

_____

Dorcas (Acts 9:39)_____

All these persons were in a right relationship with God, and this certainly affected their abilities. This is particularly striking in Joseph's case. But the ability to perform certain skills seems to go behind this to the very nature of a person himself and how God has made him. What skills or occupations did Cain's descendants (not in a right relationship with God) develop? (Genesis 4:19-22)

_____

_____

_____

This "resident ability" is considered in the New Testament when men are chosen to fulfill certain tasks in the church.

I. Read Acts 6:1-6, and then list the qualifications required for the job. Which of these would you consider in the sphere of "resident ability"?

_____     _____

_____     _____

2. Read I Timothy 3:1-7. Of the qualifications listed here for an "elder" (bishop), which abilities would you consider "resident" or built-in from birth?

_____

Thus far in this unit, little has been said about a woman's unique gifts or abilities. What significance do you see in the fact that the Bible does not say much about this?

_____

Does this suggest that women in Bible times were not as gifted as they seem to be in our day? Explain.

_____

_____

Often people have been surprised to discover they could do certain things, when at heart they felt very inadequate. How does this come out in:

Exodus 3:11, 13; 4:1, 10 _____

_____

Jeremiah 1:6 _____

_____

Esther 4:10-17 _____

_____

What in the final analysis made them do what they did?

_____

To summarize: There is built in to every woman a sense of responsibility to *do*. This is qualified to some extent by the natural talents which come to her from birth and by her position as a woman. God often lays his hand on a woman for a task for which he himself has prepared her, and under that sense of call a woman "does."

There is one other principle which is significant, and it comes out in two passages. Read them in order and then state the principle.

Psalm 75:4-7 and Luke 16:10-12

_____

_____

**how am I "doing"?**
Write a paragraph describing in some detail what you believe are your God-given, resident abilities. When you have completed this analysis, ask a close friend who really knows you to share with you what she thinks you can do. Make a list as she talks, not letting her see what you have written, and then compare your judgments.

Many men find themselves in jobs which do not particularly interest them, but which their wives have encouraged them to take. What responsibility does a wife have to encourage her husband to do the kind of work he *can* do?

_____

Some wives are restless because they believe marriage curbs their freedom to develop their personal abilities. How would/do you resolve this problem?

_____

On the other hand, how can the single woman realize fulfillment?

_____

_____

In this section, "My Relationship to Myself," what has God been saying to you?

_____

_____

_____

**extra project:**
To see God's description of a virtuous woman, read Proverbs 31:10-31. Record what most challenges you about her life.

_____

_____

_____

_____

unit

# GRASPING THE BASIC IDEAS

A woman's relationship to her husband comes next. About it books have been written, jokes told, poems penned, and dramas staged. Yet there still seems to exist a great vacuum of sound understanding about this mysterious and marvelous relationship. As long as this ignorance continues, so long will the anxiety and frustration of an unfulfilled marriage leave their marks. And those marks show!

Deep within the heart of every woman dwells the longing to be known and understood by her husband. Yet many a man openly jokes about not being able to understand his wife. Perhaps he never really tried. But maybe she failed to understand him. At the outset of this chapter, therefore, let it be clearly and unequivocally stated that whether you are at this point married or not, *you* need to know the facts. Let's look at them and see what we find about this relationship.

The Scripture contains a vast amount of truth about a husband and wife, much of which is found in the real-life situations of the real people described. Besides looking at some of these situations, we will consider three key portions of Scripture.

## GENESIS 1–3
Review these chapters again, and check below when finished.
\_\_\_\_\_ Review completed.

What *facts* concerning the relationship of man and woman do you see in the following:

Genesis 1:27 _____

Genesis 1:28 _____

Genesis 2:18, 20 _____

Genesis 2:21-23 _____

Genesis 2:24, 25 _____

_____

These facts God established at creation and therefore they are true in the "nature of things." Summarize from these facts a statement describing the relationship of man and woman.

_____

_____

_____

In Unit 3 on a woman's relationship to God (p. 25) the effects of sin were considered. But think this through again.

In Genesis 3:16 how was Eve's relationship to Adam affected?

_____

Why do you think in Genesis 3:17 God held Adam accountable for "hearkening" to his wife? (Check again on I Timothy 2:12-15.)

_____

_____

Do you feel a woman should try to influence her husband? Explain.

_____

God's promise of salvation, and therefore hope, dominates this dismal picture of the entrance of sin into the world. This hope is first seen in Genesis 3:15, but then shows up again in an illustration in Genesis 3:21. What is the illustration?

_____

_____

To summarize, God has from creation ordained certain things about the relationship of husband and wife. Though affected by sin, this relationship can be blessed when Christ is at the center of that union. Now look at two New Testament passages.

### EPHESIANS 5:22-33
After reading the passage, list the key word which characterizes the right relationship of

The wife to the husband _____

The husband to the wife _____

The reason given for this relationship essentially is (pick best answer):
_____ Man is superior to woman.
_____ Women are weak; men are strong.
_____ Marriage is to illustrate a right relationship to God.
_____ God wants it that way.
_____ Psychologically it works best this way.

Two common distortions of this passage should be cleared up. How would you answer each of these "interpretations"?

l. "Since the Scripture states a woman should obey her husband in 'everything,' when he says 'jump,' I'd better jump!"

2. "Paul was obviously writing for his day, but today husband and wife function

with equal authority. Of course, I don't expect to obey my husband. What right does he have to run my life?"

Behind this standard, God's Word lays bare the ultimate standard by which a marriage relationship is gauged. See verses 25-27, 29, and 32. Agreeing with verse 32 in the "mystery" about this, list the "principles" which you see in the Christ/church relationship which apply to the husband/wife union.

_____

_____

_____

_____

Thought Question: How would a "Christian" marriage have advantage over a non-Christian marriage in the light of the Genesis and Ephesians passages?

_____

_____

**I PETER 3:1-7**
Check this passage in at least three translations.
Versions checked:  _____    _____    _____

Summarize in a sentence or two the instructions God gives here to the wife.

_____

_____

_____

What approach does Peter provide in verses 1 and 2 for a woman with a "problem husband"?

_____

While Sarah was a very attractive woman (see Genesis 12:11), what about her pleased God? (verses 5, 6)

_____

In verses 3 and 4 is Peter implying that the outward appearance of a woman is unimportant? Explain.

_____

_____

What two descriptions in verse 7 must affect a man's attitude toward his wife?

I._____

2._____

You could write a long list of "penalties" clouding a marriage relationship if a husband and wife do not live together in a biblical manner. Where does Peter say you will notice it?

_____

**summary**
Read I Peter 3:8, 9, since the Scripture itself summarizes for us. Which of the things listed here do you consider most needed in your relationship to your husband?

_____

_____

Do you believe God is speaking to you about it? What will you do about it? When?

_____

_____

unit

DEVELOPING DISCERNMENT

The "real-life" situations in Scripture provide a wonderful opportunity to learn. In I Corinthians 10:11 what reason does God give for including these illustrations in his Word? (Check the context.)

Since we are concerned about the relationship of man and wife, it follows that we can look at some of these in the Bible and see how they demonstrate or violate the principles we have just studied. We will give primary attention, however, to the wife.

Below are listed some husbands and wives, along with the passage(s) for study. Take them one at a time, analyzing them as suggested and writing down your observations.

**ELKANAH/HANNAH** (I Samuel 1)
Characteristics of love in Elkanah

Characteristics of submission in Hannah

Weak points in their relationship

_____

_____

**AHAB/JEZEBEL** (I Kings 16:29-33; 18:1—19:5; 21:1-29)
Cite occasions when Jezebel failed as "help meet" in her home.

_____

_____

What do you consider the "root problem" in this marriage relationship?

_____

_____

**NABAL/ABIGAIL** (I Samuel 25)
Write a summary of the kind of husband Nabal was.

_____

_____

_____

_____

Write a summary of the kind of wife Abigail was.

_____

_____

_____

_____

What key lesson do you believe God is showing you in this example?

_____

_____

**JOSEPH/MARY** (Matthew 1:18-25; 2:13-15; Luke 1:26-38)
How did Joseph exercise love?

_____

_____

How did Mary exercise submission?

_____

_____

**AQUILA/PRISCILLA** (Acts 18:1-3, 18, 19, 24-26; Romans 16:3-5)
Why do you suppose God included the description of this couple in Scripture?

_____

_____

What characteristics would a wife need in order to do what Priscilla did?

_____

_____

**YOU AND YOUR HUSBAND** (Psalm 128)
Being as objective as you can, select one aspect of your role as a wife in which
you feel you excel. Illustrate, if possible.

_____

_____

Name an area in your marriage relationship as a wife which your husband feels deserves attention. Do you agree with him on this? What steps have you taken to improve it?

_____   _____

_____

_____

_____

You have become aware of needs in your husband's life. What steps have you taken to help him meet these needs?

_____

_____

### summary
Someone has said that God has given man the role of responsibility and authority, while he has given woman the position of submission and honor. Do you agree? Explain.

_____

_____

_____

_____

_____

## unit 10 COPING WITH THREATS TO MARRIAGE

Scripture describes the ideal relationship of man and wife in glowing terms. Psalm 128 begins with "blessed" and later says such a husband is "happy." The description of his wife spells contentment. We have discovered how often "love" is used in the New Testament when describing the home.

These descriptions are not vain! They are real. A godly woman has all kinds of hurdles to leap in fulfilling God's purpose, but her life—especially her home life—is not "problem-centered." It is Christ-centered. She expects to have a happy home.

Such a woman, however, recognizes Satan's attacks and does what she can to keep her home happy. The following are not necessarily problems, but "threats."

**lack of communication**
Review Genesis 2:20. Why were animals not adequate for Adam?

_____

_____

Review I Peter 3:7. What does the expression *heirs together of the grace of life* imply in terms of communication?

_____

_____

_____

From the standpoint of logic alone, if a woman is to "help" her husband, what must she know?

_____

_____

Similarly, as one responsible for the home, what must a man know concerning his wife?

_____

_____

Try to be realistic as you make a list of things a wife can do to foster good communications with her husband. List at least ten.

1. _____

2. _____

3. _____

4. _____

5. _____

6. _____

7. _____

8. _____

9. _____

10. _____

Communication has much to do with a happy and God-honoring "sex life." Read I Corinthians 7:1-6 (check in several translations) noting Paul's counsel.

Although he does not use the term "frigidity," what does he imply about it?

_____

_____

Why do you suppose God included in Scripture the descriptive communication which Isaac and Rebekah experienced in Genesis 26:8? (Check context, too.)

_____

_____

Some say that in the order of things (see I Corinthians 11:3) a man should listen to and help solve his wife's problems. He should not, however, burden her with his but learn how to share them with God. Do you agree with this?

_____

_____

_____

In summary, love involves expression—even listening. Many approach marriage as though a happy sex life leads to good communication. This study suggests that good communication leads to a happy sex life. Therefore, concentrate on good communication and see what happens!

**the sin of adultery**
It's all through Scripture! Check a concordance under the term "adultery." That's what it's called. Adultery. And it's called sin.

Of course, there are all kinds of problems which can lead to an "adding to" what God has said to keep pure. But a man and wife should not be deluded into thinking that because they are well-adjusted and happily married they are immune to this threat. Don't play with it!

You should be familiar with the biblical account of David's sin of adultery. Look carefully at II Samuel 11:1—12:25. Get the facts. God included it in his Word for a purpose.

What was going on nationally? _____

_____

What was David doing when tempted? _____

_____

What was Bathsheba doing? _____

_____


While Scripture does not indicate anything to suggest that Bathsheba planned it this way, what principle is suggested about a woman's power to arouse a man's sexual desires? (Cf. also Matthew 5:27, 28.)

_____

_____


In the light of these things and taking seriously what God says in I Timothy 2:9, how do you feel a Christian woman should determine her wardrobe?

_____

_____


Now read Psalm 51. Write a paragraph telling in your own words how you think David felt about this whole thing.

_____

_____

_____

Have you analyzed the relationships you now have with other men and checked to see that everything is on the up-and-up? Where or when may you be vulnerable? Or cause someone else a problem?

_____

_____

In summary, a notion among some psychotherapists goes as follows. If a woman is married but has a poor or meaningless relationship with her husband, that is, no love, and then she suddenly finds a mate to whom she can wonderfully relate—the real idea of biblical marriage—then surely she can divorce her husband and marry her new-found partner. The basis: her first marriage cannot really be called a marriage since love and interpersonal communion never existed. Therefore the biblical injunctions against remarriage do not apply. What do you think about this logic?

_____

_____

_____

**poor management**
In a culture where more and more wives hold outside jobs, more and more marriages are suffering. And in the highly industrialized community, involving a growing amount of travel, men are also abdicating their responsibilities toward the home. A tragic emptiness results.

In Genesis 18:19 what quality in Abraham ensured the well-being of his marriage?

_____

What quality for leadership in the church of Jesus Christ is mandatory according to I Timothy 3:4, 5, 12? Is this addressed to men or women?

_____

The Scripture therefore indicates that the ultimate responsibility for the management of the home falls upon the husband. To be biblical, he must oversee and take an interest in the family. However, the godly wife sees her role as *helping* him in this. And together they act as one. How does I Timothy 5:14 show her part in management?

_____

Consider again Proverbs 31:10-31, listing the aspects of a wife's work for which she takes responsibility.

_____

_____

_____

Some women have not had the benefit of a happy background and therefore do not know how to be good home managers. How does Titus 2:3-5 indicate they are to learn?

_____

What other great source of stability does a woman have to undergird the total management of the home? (Philippians 4:4-7)

_____

After studying the above, analyze your application of these matters in your home. What things mentioned in Proverbs 31 and Titus 2 need attention in your life?

_____

_____

_____

_____

### reversed roles

Frankly speaking, some women have married men who are poor managers. In many cases these men hold jobs where creative leadership and initiative not only do not exist but are frowned upon by either labor or management or both. In days when men largely lived on the farm, they either developed management abilities or they starved. Today the situation has changed.

A woman who is a competent manager may do the decision making in the home by herself, thereby pushing the husband out of his position of leadership (and destroying his initiative and interest). What results is a reversal of roles; she's a good leader; he lives in submission to her. No such situation is condoned by Scripture! And no woman really wants this role.

To change such a situation, which by the way has tremendous spiritual and psychological effects upon children, both husband and wife must cooperate, seeking God's help and the counsel of couples whose homes are biblical. He must learn to take the lead. She must learn to let him.

List some specific ways a wife can help her husband assume his role as head of the home.

_____

_____

_____

In the next section you will think about your relationship to children. The way to being a good mother flows from being a biblical wife. Someone has said that the only other person who can wreck a man's ife is his wife. But positively speaking, there's no greater comfort to a man in this life than a wife whose whole desire is to make him a happy and effective man. "She will do him good and not evil all the days of her life" (Proverbs 31:12).

unit

# THE ROLE OF THE FAMILY

Jesus was and is a man. In fact, he is the complete and perfect man. (He is also God.) Yet Jesus loved children. In the normal, physical sense he had none of his own, but significantly the Scripture lets us catch a glimpse of his attitude toward them.

Read slowly Mark 10:13-16. (Check a modern translation.)
_____ Check here when finished.

Why do you suppose the disciples objected to the intrusion of children into Jesus' schedule?

_____

Note Jesus' reaction:
How did he feel about the situation?

_____

What did he say in substance?

_____

_____

_____

What did he do?

_____

Personal Probe: Some families by their daily schedule operate on the premise that men and children do not mix. How do you feel about this?

_____

_____

_____

To get the true picture of a woman's relationship to her children, we must review the place of the family in Scripture.

**the role of the family**
In the order of things according to Genesis, God observed, "It is not good that the man should be alone." So he gave Adam his wife Eve, establishing the principle of marriage in Genesis 2:24.

How does this principle relate to the command God gave Adam as recorded in Genesis 1:28a?

_____

_____

This "order of things" always shows the family as the basic unit of society. Man is a social being, a "family man."

What do you find in common in the following passages:
1. Genesis 6:17, 18          4. Jeremiah 32:38, 39
2. Genesis 12:1-3            5. Acts 2:39
3. Deuteronomy 29:29         6. Acts 16:31

_____

_____

Now read Ephesians 3:15. Check another translation in order to get as clear an idea as possible of this parenthetical expression in Paul's prayer. After meditating on it, check below what you believe is most accurate.

\_\_\_\_ The family illustrates what our relationship to God should be.

\_\_\_\_ The Fatherhood of God and the brotherhood of man is the obvious idea.

\_\_\_\_ God's relationship to his people actually is a family relationship.

\_\_\_\_ The whole idea of the family was God's idea.

\_\_\_\_ The family relationship was created by God because that is the way things are in heaven.

A little later we will be looking in on some of the families recorded in Scripture, but another approach to the order of things and the place of the family can be seen in the Ten Commandments. While all of them certainly apply to the family, five actually mention some aspect of family relations. After reading over all ten in Exodus 20:1-17, note what reference is made to the "family" in each of the following:

Commandment 2 (20:4-6) _____

_____

Commandment 4 (20:8-11) _____

_____

Commandment 5 (20:12) _____

_____

Commandment 7 (20:14) _____

_____

Commandment 10 (20:17)_____

_____

Thought Question: To whom does it appear these Ten Commandments are addressed?

_____

If a woman will be a woman, she must therefore see herself as a part of a family. This may be as a wife, a mother, a daughter, or a sister. But with God's blessing, these relationships become a great part of her happiness.

Read slowly Psalm 128. In your own words write a brief summary of this description of the blessed or happy home.

_____

_____

_____

_____

**you and your family**
How would you describe your family life:
_____ unqualifiedly happy
_____ happy, what there is of it
_____ okay, but not really a big part of my thinking
_____ fair, but in need of my attention
_____ some relationships good, some poor
_____ deeply unsatisfying

What has been your *experience* in terms of the principle Jesus lays down in Luke 14:26 and Luke 18:29, 30?

_____

_____

_____

unit

A WOMAN AND HER CHILDREN

Now let's visit some of the homes in the Scripture and see what we can observe. And by the way, are you aware that visitors in our homes notice these relationships? They are very apparent. And really that's an advantage . . . if you stop and think about it.

The following passages describe certain men and their children. After reading the reference(s) listed,
**1.** Name the father and mother.
**2.** Describe in a word or two their husband/wife relationship.
**3.** Note anything outstanding, good or bad, about their relationship to their children.

Genesis 13:11-13; 19:1-38

**1.** _____

**2.** _____

**3.** _____

Genesis 25:19-28

**1.** _____

**2.** _____

**3.** _____

Exodus 2:1-10; 6:20; Hebrews 11:23

1. _____

2. _____

3. _____

Judges 13:2—14:4, 10

1. _____

2. _____

3. _____

I Samuel 1:1—2:21

1. _____

2. _____

3. _____

Job 1:1-5, 13-22; 2:9-10; 42:12-17

1. _____

2. _____

3. _____

Mark 6:12-29

1. _____

2. _____

3. _____

Luke 2:1-52

1. _____

2. _____

3. _____

Acts 16:1-3; II Timothy 1:3-5; 3:14-17

1. _____

2. _____

3. _____

**summary**
Describe briefly the most significant impression you have gained from these "visits" into these homes.

_____

_____

With which situation can you most easily identify? Explain.

_____

_____

_____

_____

_____

unit

# "FATHER KNOWS BEST"

It's true! Father does know best. And even though much of Western culture has abandoned the idea, God still "blesses" or makes happy the home where Dad takes the lead.

Two particular portions of Scripture have been saved for this place in our study for they are freighted with practical tips.

Look first at Genesis 18:19.
What word is used here to denote Abraham's relationship to his household?

_____

What relationship is built up in the life of his family?

_____

What are the results?

_____

Now look at Ephesians 6:1-4. (Compare it with Colossians 3:20, 21.)
What responsibility has God laid down for children?

_____

What negative and positive responsibilities has God spelled out for fathers?

_____

_____

What are the results promised?

_____

From our previous studies, we have picked up that God's purpose in creating woman relates directly to a father's function in leading his family. Instead of competing with him, the godly wife supports her husband, and together they work out a family "life-style" in which the children, learning and laughing, grow.

To get very practical, we must translate these principles into a program for the home. And here again we can look to the practical Word of God.

**family worship**
Read Psalm 127.
What effect can come upon children who daily join their parents in a time of family worship?

_____

_____

If you were to mention four things that should characterize a "fruitful" family worship, what would you list?

**1.** _____

**2.** _____

**3.** _____

**4.** _____

What would you suggest to the mother who knows they should be experiencing such worship as a family but whose husband feels very awkward about getting started?

_____

_____

_____

A description of our family worship is:
_____ We have never begun.
_____ We tried, but it flopped.
_____ My husband won't lead it.
_____ We practice it, but it's pretty dull.
_____ We need help to learn how.
_____ I lead it.
_____ My husband leads it, and it's going well.

One simple, yet practical, approach to family devotions keeps the focus on God, not the program. It goes like this:

> Sing to *God* (praises).
> Listen to *God* (Scripture).
> Talk to *God* (prayer).

If God has been speaking to you about this matter as you have done this study, what one thing will you do in response?

_____

Special Note: Family worship is no substitute for private and public worship. Each plays its part. For our day, it might be added that public worship is no substitute for family worship.

**general instruction**
Read Deuteronomy 6.
There are several practical tips here which ought to be noted. The first pertains to the centrality of the Word of God in all education. This is the starting point

and the point of reference. With that presupposition, review Deuteronomy 6 in terms of the educational process.

Who does the teaching? _____

When is it done? _____

Where is it conducted? _____

How is it essentially carried out? _____

_____

What threat can undermine this process? _____

_____

Now look at verses 20 and 21. What significant educational process is described here?

_____

Someone has suggested that the parent's answer here (6:21-25) essentially relates to his own personal testimony of God's having saved him. Do you agree?

_____

Have you ever shared with your children how you personally became a Christian? _____

While the term *admonition* (or instruction) *of the Lord* in Ephesians 6:4 on the surface would seem to suggest the "religious" sphere, a second thought reminds us that there is no part of the universe which is unrelated to God. And God has said that parents are responsible for their children's education.

Responsibility for compulsory education, therefore, does not essentially rest with the state (civil government), but rather with God who has commanded the learning/teaching process. The state derives its authority to educate from parents, whom God holds responsible.

What steps can parents take to determine whether their children are getting a proper education?

_____

_____

What if they find the school(s) their children attend are inadequate? What are the alternatives?

_____

_____

What if they discover the church they attend fails to train their children in *the admonition of the Lord*? What are the options?

_____

_____

These questions are tough. But parents must face them honestly. In the next chapter we will look at a woman's role as a citizen, but the road to her being a good citizen is to be a responsible woman.

**discipline**
Read Hebrews 12:1-13.
While this very practical subject can be extremely unpleasant—as Hebrews 12:11 states—yet what bold term does Hebrews 12:8 use to describe the relationship where there is no parental discipline?

_____

A deeper study into Ephesians 6:4 shows the difference in these two words *nurture* and *admonition* as translated by the King James Version. *Admonition* refers to instruction. *Nurture*, however, suggests instruction by correction, or as Hebrews 12 usually calls it, *chastening*. Modern translations usually call it *discipline*.

How do you personally feel about the saying, "Spare the rod and spoil the child"?

_____

_____

_____

The attitude of permissiveness which has gained momentum in Western culture has been bringing its fruit with it. This passage in Hebrews, quoting from Proverbs, suggests that discipline brings with it a feeling of belonging. Can you explain this in terms of so many youth wondering "Who am I?"

_____

_____

_____

Note carefully Ephesians 6:4a. List at least six things that parents can do which can provoke their children to anger.

1. _____

2. _____

3. _____

4. _____

5. _____

6. _____

What principle of discipline is spelled out in Ecclesiastes 8:11?

_____

Children will often try to work one parent against the other in matters of discipline. What safeguards would you recommend to meet this situation?

_____

_____

_____

The whole matter of discipline may be not only neglected, but also misused. What significance do you see in the terms *in the Lord* and *of the Lord* in this Ephesians passage? How do they affect discipline?

_____

_____

_____

Describe briefly some experience in your life or in training your children when discipline produced outstanding results.

_____

_____

_____

In summary, discipline is not exercised primarily because it works or fails to work, but because a father is being obedient to his heavenly Father. God says! And this approach to a child, namely, "Billy, my Father in heaven has told me to help you learn to do what I say, for it's sin for you to disobey your parents— so I must paddle you," leads to his submission and growth. That is, even the child's father is under the discipline of a higher authority—his heavenly Father.

### enjoyment
Learning to enjoy God's creation as a family largely rests with the father. Since God has given him the responsibility as head of the home and the help of his wife, he and they learn to have fun together.

Look up Proverbs 15:13 and write a paraphrase in your own words.

_____

_____


Here's a good exercise. Put down your husband's name and list one thing he really enjoys doing. Do the same for each of your children—even if it's wrestling in the back yard—and then note the date when each person last participated in this with another member of the family.

| Husband | Activity | When |
|---------|----------|------|
| _____ | _____ | _____ |
| Children | | |
| _____ | _____ | _____ |
| _____ | _____ | _____ |
| _____ | _____ | _____ |
| _____ | _____ | _____ |

Many parents, for the sake of material prosperity, are missing the time of their life . . . at home. What relationship do you see between playing with the children and their worship, instruction, and discipline?

_____

_____

_____


Children used to get the idea that the Lord's Day is a time of prohibitions. (Most children today, however, probably have lost any sense of the sanctity of the Sabbath.) What kind of a day do you think the Christian Sabbath should be?

_____

_____

What do you feel a Christian mother could do to help make the Sabbath a "delight" to the Lord (see Isaiah 58:13, 14) and at the same time enjoyable to her children?

_____

_____

Just being together doing all kinds of things . . . or nothing in particular . . . gives those natural opportunities for getting acquainted. Knowing how _you_ feel about this and that has a great part to play in your children's enjoying their parents. What does this imply about their "enjoying" God?

_____

_____

_____

**summary**
Jesus loved children. And he still does. No doubt the way to be a good mother is to seek his help every day—then to trust him. He can help us love children, too . . . and find the time to let them know it. That way it will come naturally. And happily.

unit
14 MY CHURCH

Let's review what God has been teaching us about a woman as he designed and desired her to be. You have been thinking through much Scripture. Now try to boil down one lasting impression or action resulting from your study of each of the preceding sections.

**I. Introduction (The happy woman)**

_____

_____

**II. My Relationship to God**

_____

_____

**III. My Relationship to Myself**

_____

_____

**IV. My Relationship to My Husband**

_____

_____

## V. My Relationship to My Children

_____

_____

Up to this point, we have been looking for the most part at a woman's relationships as they affect her in the "inside" of her life–the intimate relationships she experiences with herself and her family. Now we move into the area of her relationships with those outside the pale of her "relatives."

Before taking up specific considerations, we should have in view what God says about the world in which he placed woman. What do the following passages suggest about a person's general attitude toward the "world"?

Genesis 1:28    _____

Psalm 24:1    _____

Mark 16:15    _____

John 17:14-18    _____

_____

II Peter 3:10-13    _____

_____

Having this overview, a woman is now ready to consider her life and activity in various spheres of responsibility. Obviously these aspects of her life are complete studies in themselves, and we can only introduce them here. But a godly woman will keep herself in a responsible posture in these spheres. She will not be passive toward them.[1]

[1] Persons having completed this section who want to pursue certain aspects of My Relationship to Other People in its broader implications can find listed on page 115 some sources for additional study.

## my church

When you think of the "church," what *first* comes to your mind? Place a 1 in a space below to answer this. On *second* thought, what do you think of? Use a 2 to denote this.

| | |
|---|---|
| _____ a building | _____ an organization |
| _____ a minister | _____ Jesus Christ |
| _____ a fellowship | _____ a worship service |
| _____ a system of doctrine | _____ the Lord's Day |
| _____ money | _____ a graveyard |

Now read I Peter 2:9, 10. How does Peter describe the church?

What it is  _____

_____

What it does  _____

_____

Thought Question: What relationship do you see between what the church is and what it does?

_____

_____

_____

The English word "church" derives from a Greek word meaning "lord," a common term ascribing respect. Hence, "the church" essentially means the *persons* who have come to respect Jesus Christ as their King. The common word used by the New Testament writers to describe the church (*ekklesia*) means "called out ones" and forms the background of our word ecclesiastical. Both terms refer to people. How does the Bible describe:

How one gets into this "church"? (I Corinthians 1:9)_____

_____

The source of its life? (Colossians 3:1-4) _____

_____

Its relation to God's truth? (I Timothy 3:15, 16) _____

_____

How the members treat each other? (Hebrews 10:24, 25)_____

_____

Their plan for operating as a team? (Titus 1:5) _____

_____

_____

Before looking up Acts 2:42, think through and list below what you consider to be the four most basic activities of the "church." Then check your ideas with the four items listed in Acts 2:42 describing the church just after the coming of the Holy Spirit on Pentecost.

1. _____    3. _____

2. _____    4. _____

A common problem with some persons shows up in their independent spirit when it comes to the church. What attitude does Peter describe as an alternative? (I Peter 5:5)

_____

Let's look more closely at this passage. Some "independents" defend themselves by a charge that either the leaders of the church have not led . . . or that they have led them astray. In the light of I Peter 5:1-4, would you agree with their criticism? Explain.

_____

_____

If the church of today will be and do as God requires, what must be true:

Of the members? (I Thessalonians 5:12, 13) _____

_____

Of the leaders? (I Thessalonians 5:14) _____

_____

Pastors have a tough job. They must seek to fulfill a job description set up by God but not always recognized by others. How does that job show itself in:

Acts 6:1-4 _____

Ephesians 4:11-13 _____

II Timothy 2:2 _____

Now read Romans 12:3-8. What are some of the gifts God has given Christ's body (the church) for "serving"?

_____

_____

To summarize, Jesus Christ heads up his people—his church. He gives them life and by his Spirit moves among them so that they can fellowship with and minister to each other on the basis of his Word, the Scripture. He has arranged for the church to have leaders, who in turn help the people in their growth and also train them for their ministry. This ministry comes as a Spirit-given gift, and each person has at least one gift. As the people of God, they penetrate the world with a demonstration and a declaration of what it means to be in fellowship with God, thus extending God's Kingdom to every sphere of life.

**my relationship to my church**

How would you appraise your relation to the church:

_____ Generally I would rather function independently—and do.

_____ I feel the church is to "be and do" as God's witness in the world, but I don't know any such body.

_____ I joined it, but frankly it doesn't figure very high in my priorities.

_____ We have our problems, but my church is making progress and I'm available to move ahead with it.

_____ I don't really understand much about it, so my relation to it is rather weak.

What gift(s) do you believe God has given you as a member of Christ's body?

_____

_____

What training have you had in order to exercise the gift(s)?

_____

What training do you need?

_____

unit

15 MY WORK

We began this whole study by looking at the happiness or blessedness of the woman who is what God intended her to be. Now when it comes to the subject of work—one of the most important aspects of life—many persons have adopted the equation *happiness = leisure* minus *work*. Or to put it in another way: *happiness increases inversely in proportion to work.*

Read now Psalm 128, which also begins with "blessed," and note the place of "labor" in the happy person's life.
_____ Psalm 128 completed

The inference here is that there is a connection between "walking in God's ways" and "labor." To review this connection, go back and recall the following sections of this study. Check when review is completed.
_____ Man's purpose (pp. 20-22).
_____ Your most satisfying responsibility (p. 24).
_____ What I can do (pp. 47-51).

**why work?**
To the question "Why work?" one might give several answers. While all of those answers could be true, they probably would differ in importance. Below are listed a number of reasons for working. Put them in the order of priority as you see them, placing a 1 beside the most important, a 2 beside the next most important, etc.
_____ To provide financial support for myself and my family
_____ To be a good example to other people
_____ To gain a sense of fulfillment and completion
_____ To better my standard of living

_____ To carry out my purpose as God created me
_____ To provide funds to support missionary and welfare enterprises
_____ To get a job done that will help other people
_____ To get inside a situation where I can share the gospel
_____ To do the particular thing Christ called me to do

What work-related principle do you find in Jesus' life as shown in John 4:34? (Check the context.)

_____

_____

How does this same principle carry over in

Colossians 3:22? _____

_____

Colossians 4:1? _____

_____

Learning to do one's work "unto the Lord" takes in many things. Below are listed some references in Scripture involving a person and some phase of his work. Name the person and the aspect of "doing one's work to God" which you see in each.

| Scripture | Person | Aspect |
|---|---|---|
| Mark 1:16-18 | | |
| Genesis 39:7-12 | | |
| II Kings 5:20-27 | | |
| Daniel 6:3, 4 | | |
| Luke 2:36-38 | | |

Amos 7:10-15 _____   _____

Luke 19:1, 8-10 _____   _____

II Timothy 4:9, 10 _____   _____

What are the sharp warnings about work in the following references?

I Timothy 5:8 _____   _____

II Thessalonians 3:10-12 _____   _____

### my own work
Crucial in a Christian woman's sense of fulfillment is an awareness of the relationship existing between her work and the Kingdom of God—or as one person puts it, the relationship of one's "profession" to his "profession of faith." In order to grasp this relationship, a woman must answer certain questions. Answer them for yourself the best you can at this point. Be honest. An "I don't know" may be necessary. And remember, while a housewife may not consider her work under the category of a profession, nonetheless it is her work—and important. She too must learn how her work relates to the Kingdom.

What evidence do you have that God led you into your present work?

_____

_____

What Scriptures has God used to show you his purpose for you in this work?

_____

_____

How has your work affected the spreading of the gospel to all the world?

_____

_____

Have you had a sense of God's call to something/someplace else? Explain.

_____

_____

**summary**
"Prosperity" according to Scripture is not necessarily making a lot of money, nor is it simply growing in spiritual matters. It means essentially seeing God's blessing on your life as you do what he has called you to do. A woman can expect this prosperity if she is *where* God wants her and doing *what* God put her there to do.

As a result of this particular study on your work, what has God said to you?

_____

_____

_____

What will you do in response?

_____

_____

unit

# MY GOVERNMENT

When you think of the "government" what *first* comes to your mind? Place a 1 in a space below to answer this. On *second* thought, what do you think of? Place a 2 to denote this.

_____ a building           _____ a flag

_____ a uniform         _____ Jesus Christ

_____ a country         _____ a song

_____ a body of laws     _____ problems

_____ money          _____ political parties

Now read Romans 13:1-7 (use a modern translation). What does this passage say about:

The idea of "government"? _____

_____

The purpose of civil government? _____

_____

The extent to which a government may exercise its authority? _____

_____

The specific obligations of its citizens? _____

_____

The Bible purports to be God's Word, and therefore binding on a person's belief and practice. What significance do you see in the fact that the Word of God speaks concerning the "philosophy" (not the form) of civil government?

_____

_____

**church and state**
It is a common idea that religion is one thing and government is another (often termed the "church/state"* question) and "ne'er the twain shall meet." The Bible, however, speaks often and unequivocally in such a manner that one *must* consider what God says before drawing his conclusions. For example, below are some passages which use legal or governmental terms. Look up the reference, write down the governmental term, and then comment briefly on the implications.

Genesis 1:28 _____

_____

Genesis 3:16 _____

_____

Deuteronomy 1:16 _____

_____

Psalm 2:10, 11 _____

_____

Mark 1:14, 15 _____

_____

*"State" in this study refers to civil government in general, not just at the state level.

John 19:19 _____

_____

Revelation 19:16 _____

_____

God has thus spoken to both church and state and has claimed to have given Jesus Christ supreme authority over both. (Check Matthew 28:18 with Colossians 1:13-18.) The man who follows Christ will therefore obey Christ in reference to civil matters. There are three basic ways by which he does this:

**1.** Respect: Read I Peter 2:13-17 and write down a common violation of this command.

_____

**2.** Support: How did Jesus do this as recorded in Matthew 17:24-27?

_____

**3.** Participation: What position did Erastus hold according to Romans 16:23? (Check a modern translation.)

_____

Have you ever considered serving God in holding some governmental (or political) office? What position do you feel best qualified to fill?

_____

In the light of our study on husband/wife relationships, why do you think so many women are seeking public office? Do you think they should?

_____

_____

Scripture indicates there are times when one must dissent from the decisions of the government over him. Two occasions like this appear in the book of Daniel. What consequences befell the dissenters?

Daniel 3 _ _____

Daniel 6 _____

In similar fashion the apostles refused to be silenced when ordered to stop preaching the gospel. What was their reason? (Acts 4:18-20)

_____

When one reads I Timothy 2:1-6, he sees a marvelous relationship between church and state. First, the church must pray for the well-being of the state, government leaders in particular, in order that the state might maintain peace. This in turn provides the necessary environment in which the church may prosper in spreading the gospel. Do you agree with this interpretation? Explain.

_____

_____

_____

**summary**
While Scripture states that God himself has ordained government and given all authority to Jesus Christ, many persons feel Christ should be kept out of government matters. In the Constitution of the United States, for example, neither God nor Christ is mentioned. (The Declaration of Independence speaks of our Creator and Divine Providence.) Hence, the United States *as a nation* has not lined up under Christ's leadership (or "blessing"). How do you feel about this omission?

_____

_____

_____

## unit 17 MY CULTURE

It may seem strange to include a section on "culture" in this study for women. As a matter of fact many persons wonder if the subject has any connection whatever with the Bible. Regardless of how strange or new it may appear, before concluding you can skip this unit, consider what is meant by "culture." You may come up with some interesting and relevant ideas. And, after all, that is how we grow.

### the meaning of culture
Look up the meaning of *culture* in a dictionary. Since it can be defined in various ways, record what you consider to be the three most common usages.

1. _____

2. _____

3. _____

Now what has this to do with being a woman? Or perhaps a better way to put it would be to ask, How much of a woman are you? That is, some persons only develop certain aspects of their life, and the results reveal many unfulfilled and unhappy experiences.

In contrast, David describes his own "way of life" in Psalm 26:1, 11 with the term *integrity*. What do you think he means?

_____

How does your answer compare with the literal meaning of that word?

_____

The goal of a Christian woman's life can be described in one sense as becoming integrated . . . or one . . . in her total world view. But this means she must develop a "cultural" viewpoint which grows out of the roots of her relationship to God.

What do the following passages imply about a person's viewpoint?

Isaiah 6:3 _____

Ephesians 4:15 _____

_____

Colossians 1:16, 17 _____

_____

Colossians 2:3, 4 _____

_____

### the cultural mandate
Undoubtedly the most basic command of God motivating a person to be an integrated personality is the one we have looked at many times in this study: Genesis 1:28. Sometimes called the "cultural mandate," this command (mark the following true or false):
_____ was given after sin entered the world.
_____ relates to all of creation.
_____ has nothing to do with women.
_____ no longer applies since sin entered the world.
_____ only affects Christians.

As man began to multiply on the earth, two direct lines began to develop: the descendants of Cain and the children of Seth. In Genesis 4:16-22, what cultural developments can be seen in the line of Cain?

_____

_____

Were Cain and his descendants "integrated"? _____ What was wrong with their culture, demanding such terrible judgment as predicted in Genesis 6:5-7 and fulfilled in the great flood?

_____

_____

### culture in contrast
Here's an interesting contrast in Scripture: David and Nebuchadnezzar. Both wealthy kings saw cultural development under their reigns. (Babylon's Hanging Gardens were one of the Seven Wonders of the Ancient World.) But how would you note the way each carried out the cultural mandate?

I Chronicles 22:1-5 _____

Daniel 4:28-30 _____

This difference should always distinguish the descendants of Seth from the offspring of Cain. But some persons feel that to become involved with cultural development at all is unchristian. How does a comparison of Psalm 24:1 with I John 2:15, 16 relate to this idea?

_____

_____

On the other hand, some Christians "compartmentalize" their lives, acting as though Christ has little or nothing to do with their being all wrapped up in cultural interests. What light do the following passages throw on this attitude:

Colossians 2:8, 9 _____

_____

Ephesians 5:8-13 _____

_____

A particularly interesting comment about Moses can be found in Acts 7:22.
What influence do you think his early background had upon his job as leader of
Israel? (As you ponder this, review Hebrews 11:24-26.)

_____

_____

Under Moses' leadership the descendants of Seth (Israel) began to develop as a
nation and the seeds of a God-centered culture were planted. What evidences of
that culture do you see today?

_____

_____

Thus, the Christian woman sees herself in a world created by God, full of the
glory of God, and committed to mankind to subdue or dominate for God.
Having been affected by sin, however, including her own ability to perceive truth
and participate in ruling the world for her Creator, the godly woman must begin
to cultivate a comprehensive viewpoint consistent with her faith in Christ. This
takes on two basic aspects: (1) a critical analysis of her present culture and (2)
an aggressive interest in areas yet to be explored. Both of these aspects become a
marvelous avenue of Christian witness in the world.

**approaching my culture**
Where does one start? Let's be concrete. Magazines like *TIME* seek to cover the
cultural scope. The areas listed below are typical of their table of contents. Run
down the list; then number them in the order in which you feel most conversant.
("Religion" has been omitted.)

| _____ Art | _____ Environment | _____ Press |
| _____ Behavior | _____ Law | _____ Science |
| _____ Books | _____ Medicine | _____ Show Business |

_____ Business          _____ Modern Living       _____ Sports
_____ Cinema            _____ Music               _____ Television
_____ Education         _____ Nation              _____ World

Now go back and circle the ones in which you believe you are beginning to develop a Christian perspective.

Which area of our culture do you believe to be causing the greatest negative influence in our country. Explain your answer.

_____

_____

When someone uses the expression "the American way of life," what image comes to your mind, Christian or non-Christian? Explain.

_____

_____

As an insight on your own interests, what do you most enjoy doing when you have an opportunity to relax?

_____

While interests vary with individuals, the Christian woman will endeavor to live her life in terms of God's purpose for his world (that is, in terms of the Kingdom of God), and at the same time she will try to sharpen her ability to analyze her culture, enjoying those aspects which honor her Lord and testifying against those influences with roots and purposes that are pagan. To what does she ultimately look forward? (II Peter 3:13)

_____

Have you ever made a comprehensive study in Scripture of the "Kingdom of God?" _____

Are you ready to begin such a study now? _____

If so, one way to start is to check in a concordance all of the references in the New Testament to Jesus as king.

In the space below write down one area of culture which you believe God would have you explore at this time.

_____

_____

unit

**MY WORLD**

The last things Jesus said before he returned to heaven were about the world. And the upshot of it all was this: "All authority everywhere is mine, so you go and let the whole world know who I am, what I have done, and what I desire."

Read Jesus' words for yourself in Matthew 28:18-20. Check when read. _____

**the Word and the world**
According to Luke's record in Acts 1:8, Jesus simply stated as a *fact* that these men *would* get the Word out. On what basis? His authority, of course, which involved the coming of the Holy Spirit.

But Acts 1:8 also shows a pattern—that is, how this "witness" would move out. What four stages do you see?

1. _____    3. _____

2. _____    4. _____

Now list the parallel stages in your own situation.

1. _____    3. _____

2. _____    4. _____

There's a simplicity here which no person can afford to miss. To be effective in the world a woman simply starts *where* she is. And she begins in terms of *who* she is. It is Christ alone who fills her with what she needs to be a "witness." How is this shown in Matthew 4:19?

_____   __  ___ _____      _____

_____

Suffice it to say that the woman who has set herself to *follow Christ* as Christ directs her through the Scripture will be amazed to see God begin to use her. What part of John 14:21 shows this?

_____

How does this tie in with Acts 4:13?

_____

_____

Now according to Acts 4:20, what does a "witness" tell?

_____

### sharing your experience
To implement this in your life, recall the events leading up to and following your becoming a Christian. This can be done by jotting down the significant events in your life and then organizing them. Persons having had a "crisis" conversion might follow an outline like this:
1. What my life was like before
2. How God brought me to Christ
3. What it has been like since

Many Christians cannot recall an abrupt "turning around" experience, but have been aware of a personal faith in Christ since childhood. An outline for their experience might go something like this:
1. The Christian environment in which I grew up
2. The means God used to bring me to faith in Christ
3  The evidences I have seen of his blessing

Try to confine your account to significant facts, including names, places, occasions, using terminology an unchurched person would understand. (For an example of such a "testimony" read Acts 22:1-21.)

When you have finished writing it out (probably two sheets of paper longhand), read it over. Then ask a friend to listen to it and ask her for any comments or criticism. Ask yourself, "If a non-Christian were listening, could she understand from my experience what she ought to do to be saved?" Watch out for cliches and emotionally-loaded terms. Revise it if necessary, and then begin to *pray* for an opportunity to share it with someone who needs to be saved. Check the following list as you complete each step.

_____ Pray and recall your experience.

_____ Write it out following outline.

_____ Share it with a friend (a Christian).

_____ Revise/rewrite as necessary.

_____ Pray for God's opportunity.

_____ Relate it to another person.

**telling the word**
In addition to sharing one's experience, a person can learn how to present the gospel. In Luke 24:47 what did Jesus say should be preached?

_____

_____

How did Philip carry that out in Acts 8:35? _____

_____

_____

There are many passages and many approaches to presenting the gospel of Jesus Christ. The following presentation has many uses and can be extremely flexible. It is presented here in brief but can be expanded as necessary.

This presentation could be given many titles, such as "An Overview of the Bible," "The Four Main Events in History," "The Four Basic Questions a Person Can Ask."

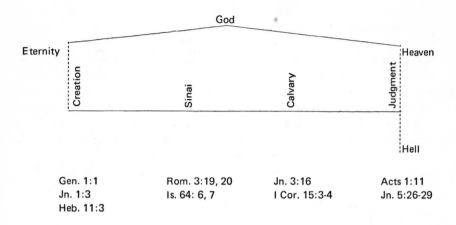

Gen. 1:1          Rom. 3:19, 20     Jn. 3:16          Acts 1:11
Jn. 1:3           Is. 64: 6, 7      I Cor. 15:3-4     Jn. 5:26-29
Heb. 11:3

Suppose we use the last title above. In explaining to a person this "time line," we begin by showing him the truth of creation, thereby answering the question "Who Am I?" The answer is obviously "a creature made by God with value and purpose."

Sinai, however, shows the sinfulness of the human heart and answers the question "What Am I Like?" My frustrations, anxieties, rebellion, etc., all stem from a heart steeped in sin. (Note: God took the initiative to show people their sin; otherwise they would have continued in it.)

Calvary is the crux of the gospel and involves spelling out the facts of Christ's life, death, and resurrection. Here the question "What Do I Need?" is answered. No mention is made at this point of belief or repentance. Only the facts are given. The point: atonement.

Finally, all history moves toward the Judgment. Thus the question "What Is Going to Happen to Me?" The answers are first given objectively: some will go to heaven, others will go to hell. No mystery here about the future.

But now we put the question personally, for in the final analysis what happens to the person will show itself in his own response. Now what will he *do* about God's sacrifice for sin? God commands him to (a) confess his sin, (b) turn to God in repentance, and (c) receive the gift of life in Christ Jesus. If he refuses, God warns him that he will perish in hell. But God calls him now to receive life.* Be sure to give him opportunity to respond.

You should think through this presentation carefully and then practice giving it. You may wish to use other references, but the diagram will help visualize God's plan of salvation. Draw it *as* you present it, using whatever you have handy. A napkin and a ballpoint pen are fine. And practice is the key to performance. Check your progress below.

_____ I have reviewed this presentation.

_____ I have practiced it.

_____ I am ready to use it.

_____ I have used it at least once.

In summary, God made man and woman to show his own glory. And when a woman becomes a Christian, God is again showing that glory. So out from her—in her own "Jerusalem"—God will send out his Word to others. How? By the woman's testimony and declaring of the gospel.

**taking action**

Below list the names of five persons you know who give evidence of a need to be saved.

1. _____

2. _____

3. _____

4 _____

5. _____

*The Scripture clearly teaches that God must save a person. In this sense, what happens to him depends alone upon God's sovereign, electing grace. However, while this should be explained to the listener, it is never the ground of appeal in presenting the gospel. The appeal is always made in terms of man's responsibility. God enables and persuades his elect to *come* to Christ. See John 6:43-45.

Will you covenant to pray for their conversion and seek an opportunity to share your testimony and/or the gospel with them? Check below if you will do it.

\_\_\_\_\_ I will pray for the conversion of the above persons, and seek to share my testimony and the gospel with them.

Certainly one of the great concerns of the Christian in the world shows itself in his alleviating human suffering. Note Jesus' example in Acts 10:38. What does it say about him?

_____

_____

However, philanthropic activities also must be tied in with the Kingdom of God. They have no intrinsic value in the sight of God apart from God's purposes. Read the parable in Matthew 25:31-46, and then decide *why* the Christian performs such activities. Record your reason.

_____

_____

_____

What inference may be drawn here regarding the person who professes to be a Christian but actually has no place in his life for these acts of mercy?

_____

_____

Are you presently engaged in any organized effort to alleviate human suffering or injustice? Explain.

_____

_____

_____

Note: Section VI (composed of the last five units) has dealt with certain areas which all too often have been neglected. Persons desiring more detailed information on a Christian viewpoint applied to the world situation may write:

Association for Public Justice
Dr. James Skillen, c/o Gordon College
255 Grapevine Rd.
Wenham, Mass. 01984

Committee for Justice & Liberty
229 College St., Toronto, Ontario M5T 1R4

You may not agree with everything these organizations are promoting, but they should challenge you to take a deeper interest in contemporary politics and cultural matters.

You will find the books of Francis A. Schaeffer both stimulating and satisfying. They not only set forth a Christian viewpoint but also lay bare the contemporary counterpart as seen in humanism. *The God Who Is There, Escape from Reason, Death in the City* and *The Church at the End of the 20th Century* (all published by InterVarsity Press) will get you started.

unit

# WHEN A WOMAN BECOMES A WOMAN

When a woman becomes a woman, she begins to make mature judgments and exercises self-control in line with those judgments. For a Christian, those judgments are based on the Word of God. Hence, the study concludes on the same note with which it began. The "happy" or blessed woman maintains a daily relationship with God through the Scriptures. But she must know how to *use* them.

Two methods of Bible study which can be very helpful to such a woman are the "topical" study and the "character" study. Below are listed some instructions for working both, along with some suggested subjects to continue a lifelong plan of "meditation."

## a topical study

**1.** Select your topic, deciding upon a word or synonyms.

**2.** Using a concordance, select the passages of most significance, probably 20 or 30.

**3.** Group the passages into logical categories. (This can be done in a number of ways: They often group themselves as you ponder them. "What, why, where, when, etc." often work well.)

**4.** Write down any problems encountered in the study. (Pursue these in later study.)

**5.** Write a paragraph summarizing what the Scripture says about the subject.

**6.** Write a personal application:

    a. What has God told me to believe or do?

    b. How have I been failing in this?

    c. What will I do about it?

Here are some "topics" as starters:

| | | | |
|---|---|---|---|
| Patience | Holiness | Faith | Fear |
| Truth | Power | Pride | Love |

**a character study**
1. Select the person to be studied.
2. Using a concordance, list the passages to be considered.
3. After meditating on the portions, write a 100-word character sketch of the person.
4. List his weak points.
5. List his strong points.
6. List problems encountered in the study. (Pursue these later.)
7. Write a personal application:
   a. What has God told me to believe or do?
   b. How have I been failing in this?
   c. What will I do about it?

The following women can provide a basis for a helpful character study, yet do not require the use of extensive or scattered passages.

Ruth—Ruth 1—4
Hannah—I Samuel 1—2:21
Athaliah—II Chronicles 22—23
Esther—Esther 1—10
Elizabeth—Use a "Harmony of the Gospels"

*Charm is deceitful, and beauty is vain: but a woman who fears the Lord is to be praised.* (Proverbs 31:30)